C.A.R.E.
to Make a Difference

C.A.R.E.
to Make a Difference

(a simple and effective
experiential learning framework
for educators)

Murray   Leadbetter   Koller

www.ihubcollective.com

·Murray, S., Leadbetter, R., Koller, A.
C.A.R.E. to Make a Difference: A Simple and Effective Experiential
Learning Framework for Educators

Published by: iHub Collective
www.ihubcollective.com

Illustrations: Agnes Koller
Book Layout & Cover Design: Agnes Koller / figdesign.ca
Cover photo: Federico Caputo / depositphotos.com

ISBN 978-1-7782081-1-9

Contents

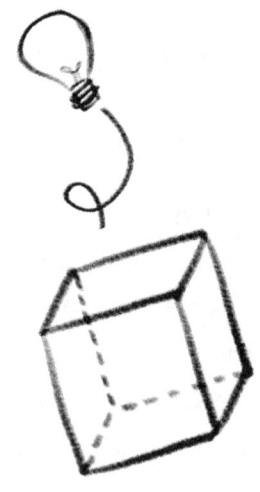

INTRODUCTION

CHAPTER 1

C.A.R.E.—A simple lever to open big doors

The Cycle of Active Relevant Engagement (C.A.R.E.) is an easy-to-use experiential learning method. It has been researched and refined over several years with hundreds of teachers and from volumes of academic research on learning. C.A.R.E. is perfect for quickly and effectively generating the structures and conditions for deep learning, metacognition, reflection, and quality feed-back, among other things important to a solid education.

And these are just the highlights—there is much more to unpack in the following pages.

Most importantly, C.A.R.E. is an impactful, effective method complete with instructions, resources, and guidance. C.A.R.E. will give you a sturdy foundation to rest upon as you move your teaching and learning into the realm of experiential, relevant, and authentic practice.

The C.A.R.E. method is outlined in the diagram below (see Appendix A for a larger version). It is practice-proven and easy to implement in schools and classrooms. In this book, we will show you how it can bring together (i) core curriculum with (ii) essential competencies and (iii) meaningful learning opportunities based in the local community. This is a trifecta win for students, and as you will see, also for teachers.

Cycle of Active Relevant Engagement
(C.A.R.E.)

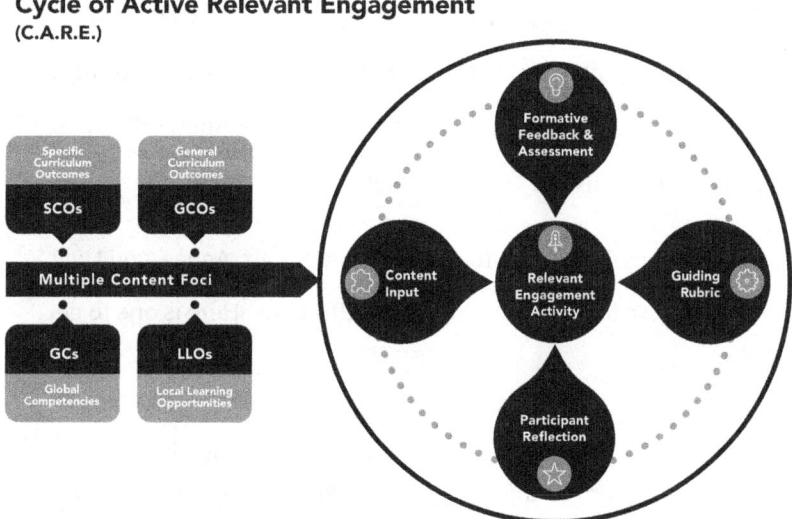

Through our highly acclaimed not-for-profit Innovation Hub (iHub) we have tested C.A.R.E. with hundreds of teachers and thousands of students over the 2018–2019, 2019–2020, 2020–2021, and 2021–2022 school years. And it works!

C.A.R.E. works so well that educators in our community will gladly tell you it provides a solid, proven way to generate the authenticity, relevance, and engagement essential to creating deep and enduring learning. Furthermore, we have practical resources and support ready for you and your colleagues to engage with and benefit from—we are here for you beyond the pages of this book!

Additionally, it is important to put it right out front: the C.A.R.E. method provides solid, useful, and relevant assessment you can use for all types of formative and summative accounting of grades. You will be happy to know the C.A.R.E. method makes assessment quick, easy, and targeted.

Testimonials are easy to come by, and Stuart, Agnes, and I will give you a lot of those throughout this book. Here is one to get started:

> *"As always, iHub has pushed me out of my bubble and allowed for this unique opportunity to further develop my teaching style. Innovative Education is our future*

but sometimes it is hard to incorporate into our teaching day. This opportunity has opened my eyes to see how rewarding and successful it can be."

We will provide you with a detailed description of each step involved in the C.A.R.E. model. In the meantime, the graphic organizer (on page 9) presents the model in brief. As you can see, the foundation of C.A.R.E. rests upon multiple inputs, which help determine the outcomes being sought and the direction a learning endeavour will take. Of central importance is the chosen activity. Along with the desired outcomes, the activity is used to co-develop the guiding rubric (Appendix B) that will organize learning and guide progress. The guiding rubric is essential for helping students demonstrate competency and growth as they work to achieve the goals set out by using reflection and assessment tools.

We are confident C.A.R.E. will genuinely support your teaching practice. Best of all, the intuitive framework will help ensure that learning endeavours are efficient, effective and meaningful for both you and your students.

A Brief Introduction of the Authors

My name is Dr. Ross Leadbetter—I hold an interdisciplinary doctorate in knowledge creation, conversion, and high-performance teaming. I have been working in and around public education, university education, coaching, leadership development, and organizational improvement for over 30 years now.

My co-collaborator, Stuart, is a *youngish* teacher with amazing ambition to make a difference in our world through education. He has worked in a variety of classrooms, has transformed many young lives with experiential learning, and he is currently coaching numerous teachers in the C.A.R.E. method. He is also a burgeoning small-scale-sustainable farmer and an inspiration to our profession.

Agnes came on board after we had had the chance to field test C.A.R.E. with several teachers in diverse classrooms. Her background in teaching is grounded in nature-based and Waldorf -inspired education. With experience working in both the public and private school sector, Agnes provides an informed perspective on the value of holistic, place-based education.

The three of us will tell the story of C.A.R.E. and outline a path you can travel to implement C.A.R.E. in your schools and classrooms. We are keen to help you to transform your teaching and learning while using your current curriculum, the global competencies, and local learning opportunities as the critical components of deeply authentic and enduring learning.

Of note: though Stuart, Agnes and I are equal contributors in this work, I will generally write about C.A.R.E. on a macro level. You will hear Stuart's voice in many of the front-line examples of the method in action, and Agnes' in the nature-based education perspective as well as the wonderful accompanying graphics. We hope you find our writing styles are a good balance of academic rigour and practical application mixed with a passion for educational innovation, and, hopefully, fun, and entertaining.

Learning is serious business, but a bit of fun can go a long way. As Dr. William Glasser is fond of telling us, people react well and do well when they are safe, belong, have power, and are able to experience freedom and fun. That is what we believe the C.A.R.E. method helps achieve too: it helps schools and teachers create safe, unifying, empowering, liberating, and fun learning environments. Enjoy!

CHAPTER 2

The learning trap

Getting Out of the Gate & Meeting Challenges Head On

In the following discussion, I set up an argument for using the C.A.R.E. method by pointing out the folly of some assumptions and practices that school systems and society accept about education.

None of these assumptions are malicious or intentionally misguided. However, they have the effect of creating anxiety, behaviour problems, boredom and much more—none of which is helpful to the pursuit of authentic, relevant, and engaging learning.

Please come with me on a brief tour of these topic areas and notice how we position the C.A.R.E. method to work *within* the current boundaries created by these assumptions and practices. That is correct. It is important to note that to use C.A.R.E. effectively, you do not have to 'break down' anything.

In this book, we will show how you can use C.A.R.E. immediately—right now—to create important and essential structures and conditions needed in your school and in your classroom to develop enthusiastic, engaged students who can and will experience deep and enduring learning.

Now, let's get going and walk through some of the assumptions impeding education.

THE ELEPHANT IN THE ROOM

So, let us first examine the biggest question and challenge of all: are education systems and classrooms everywhere currently **engaging** and serving all our students?

No.

No, they are not. And there is plenty of research to support this statement.

So... curriculum—is it the problem?

No, curriculum is not the problem. We have seen standard curriculum used in the C.A.R.E. method to ignite the curiosity of students. It has helped teachers move through curriculum like a hot knife through butter, all while motivating and invigorating their students to learn.

Students? Are they the problem?

No.

No, they are not.

We have seen the C.A.R.E. method help motivate apathetic, confrontational, and disengaged students, who have come alive and become curious about the world around them. We have seen students re-engage with learning, demonstrate their innate talents, and develop their skills and abilities while dramatically decreasing all types of behaviour problems.

So—No—students are not the problem.

At least not when we use the C.A.R.E. method.

So, what is the biggest problem with education?

Here it is—it is simple: our systems of education have not thought for a long time now—as a system—about the core purpose of education:

Learning

This is it. The biggest problem in education—the elephant in the room—is that education has lost its way.

What are we hoping to achieve through learning? Although learning is the core process of education and the core responsibility of teachers, education has become accountable to an accountability process not based on deep and enduring learning!

It is no wonder engagement with school is so low. Learning is not being held at the centre of our collective practice. Yes, education has become accountable to an accountability process. Have a look at how this plays out in the next section—'the information trade'.

THE INFORMATION TRADE

Learning is natural. It is how humans as a species have survived and thrived for millennia. It is something we will need to do proficiently as we all proceed into an ever-changing future.

Yet, what is often called learning in schools is not learning at all. What is often called learning is actually conformity to a process I call 'information trading' or 'the information trade'.

In my seminars, I often use a coffee cup to bring this example home. Here is how it works: I look in the cup, and say, "This coffee here in this cup is what I have to teach you" and then I place the cup in front of someone and say "Now, you give me this back when I ask." And, for the most part, people stare back at me blankly. Then, I say, "Okay, it is test time, give me back the cup." They do. Then I look into it and see that what I gave them is still there (no-one has yet drank my coffee!) and then I say, "Well aren't you clever! —Well done. You gave me everything back I gave you, so you get a star!"

The point is that a process occurred, but authentic learning did not. Coffee, in my example, represents the information routinely given out to students in an effort to create learning. We 'give out' information in lectures and get it back on tests. This does not create real learning, however.

But, the students who see the benefits of remembering this information and retaining it for test-time, they give it back. This exchange is the 'information trade' and it is exactly what makes school so 'dis-' or 'un-' engaging for so many students.

In fact, by the time students who are still in school reach their 11th and 12th years, 66% of them are **not** fully engaged with school. And, it is my experience, supported by research, that the lack of

student engagement is due to processes in school, like the information trade, which do not create deep and enduring learning.

Schooling and teaching through lectures and tests and work-
sheets and drills is in large part a 'forced process' easy to measure
and account. It is useful to sort students by percentages having
nothing to do with deep and enduring learning.

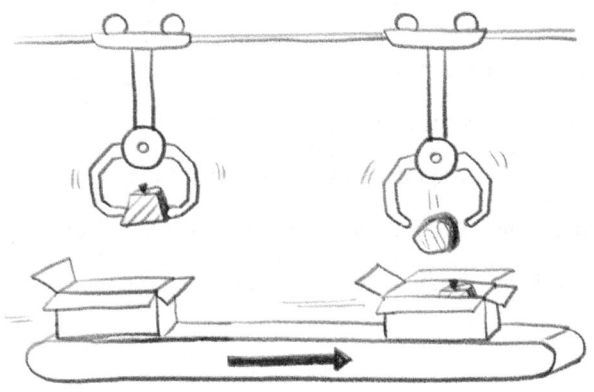

The information trade is a process—let that sink in. It is not, nor
does it create deep and enduring learning. It is an accounting
process providing numbers to regulators who can then say 'this
person is smart and this person is not.' Well, that's simply not
accurate.

Furthermore, the information trade is a process rewarding students who can sit still, listen well, retain information, and regurgitate it on a test. It does not reward our natural human need to engage with an environment and a topic in authentic, relevant, and engaging ways.

There are lots of clever people who need to engage, in a multi-sensory way, with their environment in order to learn! Think of inventors, tradespeople, entrepreneurs… And think for a second how teachers learn their craft—hands-on, in an authentic classroom setting highly relevant to their future professional work. Teachers learn their craft through an immersive, engaging activity we typically call a practicum. Is this not ironic?

The information trade is not a process of learning; it is an accounting process for education writ large. It is focussed on conformity and memory, and it is disguised as learning.

As human beings, we must strive to create knowledge if we are to experience deep and enduring learning. Knowledge is what we carry around with us—within us—the stuff we really know. I personally remember very little about any lecture I have ever attended, particularly the ones in school. I do remember activities, however. I remember building and creating and solving problems and asking really cool questions. And, if you read the research on this topic or just ask a kid—or yourself—you will notice that knowledge is created through experiences which create deep and enduring learning.

As human beings digest, ruminate over, use, and work with information it *becomes* knowledge. This is the trick to C.A.R.E. —a fundamentally human way to create knowledge is to vigorously use and experience information until it becomes embedded through learning *as* knowledge.

Knowledge is enduring. Information is not. Knowledge sticks and stays with us and is useful. Information is just information; it has no value until it is transformed into knowledge through human action and interaction.

ACCOUNTABILITY

While learning is natural for humans, something changed when modern schools were invented circa 200 hundred years ago. This most recent model of schooling is, in North America, based on an industrial standard which—a long time ago—did the job of creating life-long employees who did what they needed to do to hold a job in a factory or business.

A harrowing point here is that the path of life-long employment doesn't exist anymore—at least not for most industries or for most people.

Besides, does our modern world need more conformity or more creativity?

We must ask ourselves: do the demands of complex and intercon-nected challenges require our students now and in the future to think and act critically? Or, does our species need more people who can blindly follow old axioms and platitudes?

That brings us to another aspect of the central problem of education not focussing on learning: education systems and society have placed the wrong accountability structure on schools and classrooms. Our collective thirst for 'accountability' in education has given us an inaccurate measure.

Education systems (and society) demand that educators measure the information trade as if it were deep and enduring learning. However, it is easy to see that typical tests and exams account for the memorization and regurgitation of information and little more. This is accountability to a process of accountability rather than to learning.

Why or how this has happened to education is irrelevant right now. What is relevant right now is how we can rescue learning from it.

That is where
C.A.R.E. saves the day!

Importantly, however, the accountability to time demands, bubble answer sheets, and fill in the blanks etc. can still be done (if we must) while making what happens in our classrooms authentic, relevant, and engaging. You can still 'play the game' which has been set up, but also ensure deep and enduring learning for your students.

Please note we have been very careful in the building of C.A.R.E. and have created something that works now, within the current structures and conditions of education. When we developed C.A.R.E., we figured it is better to act now within an imperfect system than to wait for the system to become perfect before taking action.

CHAPTER 3

The purpose of education & our message of hope

Summing Up the Hard Stuff

What is the purpose of education? Is it a sorting process based on tests and scores? We hope not, but it may be only that in many cases. While there are many ways to define the purpose of education, we like to think it is (or should be) an active process empowering students to think about topics, explore ideas, create new things, connect with the curriculum, connect with others, and connect with their environments while they develop deep and enduring knowledge and skills they will carry with them their entire lives. Additionally, we think the purpose of education is to help students learn to self-start, self-regulate, and collaborate, etc. There is more too, like helping students to connect with their own power and wisdom and helping them to develop their self-esteem, self-efficacy, and locus of control… You get the idea—we believe purposeful education is active, empowering, and develops important skills and knowledge, among other things.

In short, we think education should help students think, explore, create, connect, and grow through meaningful, empowering and transformative experiences.

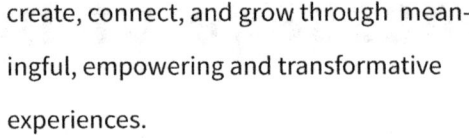

Einstein is often credited with having said: "Everybody is a genius. But if you judge a fish by its ability to climb a tree, it will live its whole life believing that it is stupid." Whoever said it, this is a great quote. To follow the metaphor, C.A.R.E. is a method that lets fish swim, monkeys

climb trees, leopards run and so on. C.A.R.E. focuses on learning first and creates a whole host of positive benefits as a result.

Let's look at it another way: if teaching does not produce deep and enduring learning, then it is not teaching, it is talking or droning, or trading information. This is a fact: if what we 'teach' does not stick and does not last, then it was never learned and is just information that comes and goes. Real learning creates knowledge, and knowledge, by definition, sticks and lasts and is useful for a lifetime.

If the subjects we teach and our teaching practices are not authentic, relevant, or engaging then most of our students will not learn well and will not want to do well. In addition, teachers will have to struggle with behaviour problems and motivate bored and disengaged students.

OKAY—Enough

That is the hard stuff done. The points are made. Let's get back to hope and our way forward.

Hope Is Not Lost—In Fact, We See Hope Today!

The C.A.R.E. method will give you the framework you need, the steps to follow, and the safety of research and practice that will allow you to become part of the great hope to transform education across the globe. By joining us, you are part of an important movement.

With the C.A.R.E. method we promote active, relevant, place-based, and engaging learning for our students, first and foremost. Knowledge is what we seek for ourselves and our students and the C.A.R.E. method is a solid path to knowledge creation and knowledge conversion which is simple, logical, practical and safe.

Additionally, as stated earlier, C.A.R.E. gives you ample assessment measures for reporting (accounting) while simultaneously giving deeply meaningful feedback to students and teachers alike. C.A.R.E. promotes deep and enduring learning while providing top-notch assessment.

That is a good balance.

VISION

We believe education is, or should be, at the centre of hope for humanity and we want to help with that hope through our belief in C.A.R.E.

At the foundation of it all is this: although current education systems are far from perfect, we can work with them and within them to create authentic, relevant, and engaging classrooms effectively serving students and teachers by creating meaningful, purposeful, deep learning. We can find our way to better learning—and we must!

WHY

Why did we write this book, and why have we researched the C.A.R.E. method for years and years? Our *why* is to help all teachers be successful in achieving deep and enduring learning. We would love to see all classrooms all over the world full of engaged students who are motivated, able, and ready for the future.

WHAT

In hundreds of research studies of our own and in studies from around the globe, we have worked with and learned from real teachers to distil the C.A.R.E. method. And, it is an approachable way to bring active, relevant, and engaging knowledge-creating learning to your systems and into your classrooms.

HOW

In this book, we are going to show you how to implement the C.A.R.E. method in your schools and classrooms.

We will show you in detail and with examples, how to bring the very best learning structures into the classroom, quickly and with very little risk. We will show you how to do it with high success from the very beginning.

*And, yes, existing curriculum is one of the core inputs in this method. So, keep your curriculum as it is for now—maybe it needs to change someday, but we are getting started today.

WHEN

To borrow from an age-old saying, here's one adapted to education: *"the best time to dramatically change teaching practices to learning practices was 20 years ago, the second-best time is today."*

And remember, you get to do all of this without 'breaking down' or destroying the old system.

WHO

There are multitudes of teachers and schools, and entire systems who everyday are managing their curriculums in new and creative ways, who are working collaboratively to develop and set common agreements and commitments with colleagues, and who are developing and targeting expectations relevant to our students and to the modern world as it exits, both today and in the future.

These are the adaptive innovators, the disruptors, the agents of change who are transforming their learning and their educational systems. Be one.

WHERE

Wherever you are, wherever you teach, rural, city, mountain top or valley floor... C.A.R.E. works where you are right now.

Diving Off the Deep End?—We Will Have None of That!

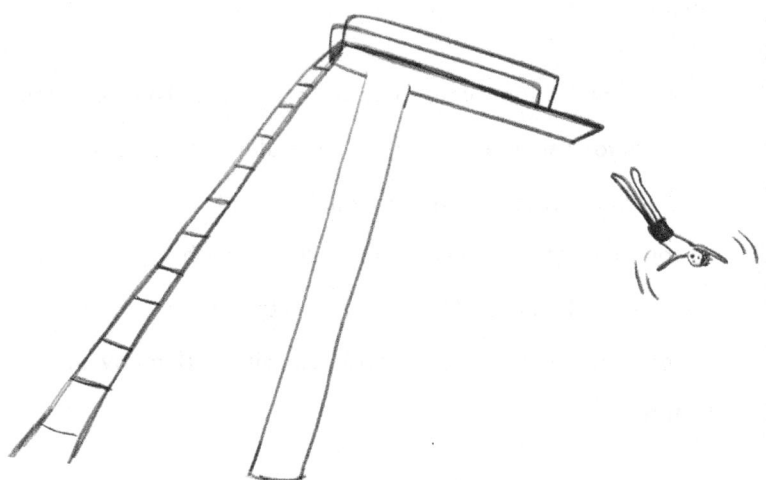

Diving off the deep end is something we think of as full of panic and frantic paddling. No one wants to do that. So, we designed the C.A.R.E. method and the implementation steps associated with it in a way that allows you to dip your toes in and get the feel of what works before committing entirely to it.

We are going to take it slow. We will walk you through practical examples and real experiences, and show you how to start a dramatic change in your practice—all with very little risk.

We think bringing power to your practice should feel good.

The **Cycle of Authentic Relevant Engagement** and all of the support we have placed around it and around you is exactly the first step you need to take to help your students:

Master the curriculum

Develop essential
competencies like
cooperation, collaboration
& critical thinking

Focus on the relevant
opportunities and challenges
of our modern world

Become motivated
& engaged

Decrease behaviour problems

The central elements of C.A.R.E. work and have worked in over 400 research studies we have conducted over the past three years—and we are still working with teachers right now, today. It is quick and easy to learn, and has solid structure. C.A.R.E. will help you to make your educational output authentic, relevant, and engaging for your students.

Yes! You can also use C.A.R.E. to prepare for high-stakes tests!

AN INVITATION

Rejuvenate curriculum, empower, and engage students, decrease behaviour problems, and easily incorporate essential competencies and meaningful learning opportunities rooted in the local community into everything you do.

Teaching is only powerful if it creates inspiring and enduring learning. Let us show you how we do it, how we teach others to do it, and how a growing community of C.A.R.E. practitioners are emerging across the globe. Enjoy the ride. We are!

CHAPTER 4

C.A.R.E works & here's the evidence

E.S.A.P.—the Early Roots of C.A.R.E.

ROSS: In 2017, I had a great opportunity to make a big change in education. I was asked to lead a small team of learning specialists who would be responsible for writing a new personalized, experiential learning program for students across our province. The goal was to serve students who were looking for a different—personalized, hands-on, relevant, and authentic—pathway to graduation than the regular high-school program offers. We were tasked with building this program and fitting it to the students rather than fitting students to a program. This was a progressive task and we rose to the challenge!

Our research showed us (and still does) that there are a lot of students who are not interested in going directly to university (or ever going to university). However, they are bright and motivated and would like to go to college, or directly to an apprenticeship, or straight to work to become chefs, early childcare workers, electricians, mechanics, hotel managers, crane operators... and more.

Our job was to create individualized pathways for these students. Thus, we developed a personalized, hands-on, self-paced program to serve them, starting with students in the 10th grade of a 12-grade public-school program. We designed it so the students who selected the Essential Skills Achievement Pathway (E.S.A.P.) pilot program would 'opt out' of most regular high-school programming and learn in a self-guided manner. These students were led by one central teacher who would help them navigate through their program and gain the skills needed to self-direct, monitor progress, and demonstrate their learning in ways closely related to their college and future interests.

The E.S.A.P. program was designed to last for three years in total (grades 10, 11, & 12). Once finished, students would be ready for college (or job opportunity, apprenticeship, etc.) to start a skilled or technical trade, business venture, vocation, etc.

The story goes like this: we had it all set up and our first schools were coming on-board starting in the fall of 2017. There was a lot of pressure to succeed. We were (and still are) completely committed to serving 'everyone' in education and providing opportunities to those students who are chronically under-served by public education – the ones not directly on a university pathway.

Sounds good, right?

E.S.A.P. addressed a lot of challenges for students who are smart and able, but who just don't see or care much about the regular programming in schools. We had gathered up excellent teachers, provided them ample training, and had got together our first batch of motivated students. At first, we were off to a very good start.

But then, about two months into our pilot program, it started to slide backwards.

Teachers were overwhelmed and kids were stuck. Each E.S.A.P. classroom could have up to 15 students on different pathways— each with different personalized learning needs. Students were idling, waiting, and depending on their teachers to know what to do next. This was not what we wanted. We wanted to create self-starting problem solvers who could tackle challenges, who could learn to perform skills at high levels of proficiency, and who could demonstrate their learning in a performance-oriented environment while giving and getting quality feedback.

Well, without going through every bit of the set up and all the challenges we faced and overcame in this program before it took off, I will share with you what is relevant to this book.

Spoiler alert, we overcame everything, succeeded with the pilot and now E.S.A.P. is successfully operating in nearly every high school in our province. And, for my personal development as an educator, I learned some amazingly powerful lessons which eventually led me to create the C.A.R.E. method with the input of hundreds of excellent educators.

Okay, back to the story of our early challenges: (i) teachers were overwhelmed with demands, and (ii) students were idling—dependent on their teachers to know what to do next.

So we started problem-solving. We brainstormed, thought things through, and kept bureaucracy out of it. We learned from and collaborated with teachers both locally and across the province.

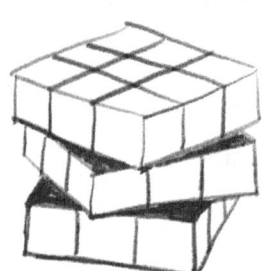

First and foremost, we knew we had to get students to understand how they could self-start an activity or a project and then how they could self-assess their progress. We knew if we could establish this pattern, we were well on our way to shifting each teacher from being the instruction-giver into the role of facilitator and guide.

We did it! We used an approach very similar to C.A.R.E.. We taught students how to 'see' the outcomes they were trying to demonstrate and how to break them down into achievable steps. We had students pick good challenges and activities which would help them demonstrate success. Further, we showed students the material they were expected to learn, and we took time to help them decode and understand the content of their personalized curriculum. Finally, we worked on feedback. Students were given the opportunity to provide feedback to others, make comments on their own learning, and they were coached on how to give and receive good feedback.

Essentially, each part of the C.A.R.E. method was built and used—over and over again until we created a clever system where students were (and still are) in charge of their learning. The key components of the E.S.A.P. system were to have students:

» See and understand outcomes

» Plan achievable steps—and take them

» Pick good challenges and activities which offer an authentic learning opportunity

» Recognize learning outcomes and know how to achieve them

» Give and receive good feedback

It was in our initial 'failure' of E.S.A.P. that the future success of the program was firmly established. And it was in this same failure and response that the seeds of C.A.R.E. were also planted.

iHUB and the Formation of C.A.R.E.

Another stroke of good fortune: in May of 2018, I was asked by our Deputy Minister of Education and visionary, Chris Treadwell, to create and head up a not-for-profit organization dedicated to the task of 'innovating education'.

< Innovating Education >

Can you relate? I am not certain about your jurisdiction, but in so many I know of, the top bureaucrats are completely out of touch with educational reality and societal needs. They are only interested in walking backwards into tomorrow, repeating what they did yesterday and calling it progress. These are the same bureaucrats supporting the 'information trade' because it gives them something easy to measure and helps them 'prove' their efforts to run education. These are the same top bureaucrats who try to apply efficiency measures and programs to education! What about value addition versus cost cutting and efficiency? Does society need efficient education or effective education? For me, the answer is clearly: "let's add value and increase effectiveness while focusing on learning."

The terrible problem in the education system is these out of touch 'leaders' are supporting inauthentic, irrelevant methods having nothing to do with modern educational research. They are looking to cut budgets when they should redirect cash towards improving learning.

How about let's get 100% of students engaged in education?

Spoiler alert, as soon as Chris Treadwell retired, a seething wave of conformity and bureaucracy crashed down on our system and is even now threatening to wash away all his amazing visionary work. Sigh. However, the silver lining is we got tons of excellent data and changed the lives of thousands of students before Chris retired. We accumulated three excellent years of data and learning to lean on and have proven the value of the C.A.R.E. method hundreds of times—all with excellent success.

So, short story: I took on the task of creating the aforementioned not-for-profit organization—iHub Learning Inc., which I led as President and CEO through three excellent years. This allowed for extensive classroom research using an active learning method: essentially C.A.R.E. in its first form.

Notably, since its inception, iHub has been able to support and research 437 projects involving over 17,500 students. Here are excerpts from some of our many reports on how our first version of C.A.R.E. changed learning in hundreds of schools and classrooms:

> *"One take away from this project was that students continued to be engaged and excited from the moment we started to the moment we finished. I was able to offer students multiple tools to complete their projects when they otherwise would not have the means to complete their ideas. They were free to use, explore and create their prototypes and designs because the tools were at their hands. It was an amazing experience to watch from start to finish."*

"I saw a positive impact on student engagement due to this project."

"I would love to keep moving forward with these projects and be more open to taking risks in my K-1 classroom. They are never too young! I have a really strong feeling that by incorporating more of these projects in my classroom I will not only see it benefiting my high fliers, but also allow my struggling learners to reach their potential by exposing them to multiple ways of learning."

"Teaching and learning does not need to be confined to the classroom. I realize this is obvious to YOU, but for teachers the four walls of the classroom can be perceived as the safest place from which to teach. Innovative Education calls on teachers to step out of their comfort zone and embrace the myriad of opportunities waiting for them beyond that traditional definition of a classroom. Thank you for this amazing learning opportunity."

"PBL and personalized learning opportunities like this one help to develop grit with our students as well as leadership skills. By allowing our students choice and voice with their learning, there is far greater buy-in and engagement from them."

Yes. All of that good messaging and goodwill with the C.A.R.E. method we are showing you in this guidebook.

Home Learning with C.A.R.E.

So, what happened in 2020 when many of us across North America and the world were forced out of the classroom for the first time? The situation gave us an opportunity to test the effectiveness and portability of the C.A.R.E. method. How did public school students—using our first version of C.A.R.E.—manage with home-based learning compared to other students?

We did the research in April and May of 2020 through on-line interviews. We're happy to report that the feedback was overwhelmingly positive! Here are just a few of the comments from interviews with educators across the province and beyond, about C.A.R.E. as a learning method:

> *"Students who already had purpose and had a reason to get over hurdles are doing well. C.A.R.E. offered choice and flexibility."*

> *"Plans and aspirations are driving engagement. Parents were happy with the structure and accountability CARE provided."*

> *"Projects and ideas that were already underway are still working."*

> *"Those students whose ideas 'had roots' before they*

left the classroom (past ideation) are moving along like nothing has changed."

"Students are able to break down tasks and talk about outcomes."

"The SYSTEM is the benefit."

"They know the OPERATIONS necessary to start, complete, and evaluate a task."

"The WHY is built in."

"The average student has to wait to be given material and then wait to have it assessed, but students using C.A.R.E. can self-start and self-assess, once they are used to the method."

"Continuous learning is built in."

There we have it. These are real teachers talking about this work—even before we refined it and built it more robustly as it is now. As you can see, the C.A.R.E. method you are learning about in this book has a lineage of success. It is an easy, accessible method for teachers and students who are looking for deep, authentic, relevant, and engaging learning.

THE C.A.R.E
PROCESS

CHAPTER 5

Inputs, meaning, and assessment

Inputs to C.A.R.E

We will begin this section of the book by talking about the inputs we choose for the C.A.R.E. method. We refer to these throughout this book. We use at least three types of input every time we use the C.A.R.E. method: curriculum, essential competencies, and meaningful learning opportunities rooted in the local community.

These input choices do 3 very important things. They:

» check the need to cover the curriculum;

» deliberately focus learning on critical competencies students need to thrive in a ever-changing future;

» focus learning on real-world opportunities to get involved that exist in our local communities—what could be more important than authentic problem-solving?

We figure that students are our hope for tomorrow—as future collaborators and creative dreamers—so why not motivate them to think critically, ask questions and address real challenges today?

To be clear, you can use any curriculum with C.A.R.E., any set of competencies, and you can focus on any real-world local learning opportunities! Below, you will see the choices we are making. We wanted you to know these up front so as to provide a glimpse into how to get started with C.A.R.E..

C.A.R.E. is not prescriptive and it is very adaptable.

First, we choose to use any curriculum, but like to use the most reduced, global, general outcome oriented —lean curriculum— possible. Lean curriculums are sprouting up all over the world and you should be able to find yours if it exists. If you do not yet

Inputs to C.A.R.E

have a lean curriculum in your jurisdiction, then use the general outcomes, or general learning outcomes—however it is phrased—and go from there. Specific outcomes are great, too, we just like to keep the big picture up front as it helps students to develop the agency and empowerment they need to be successful.

Second, we use an established set of essential global competencies developed by the ministers of education in Canada: critical thinking and problem solving; innovation, creativity, and entrepreneurship; learning to learn/self-awareness and self-direction; collaboration; communication; and citizenship These are a great set of competencies, but you can use another set. We just want to keep things simple and want to use quality frameworks that are already built because we think it helps when getting started. Your call.

Third, the real-world challenges we address are everywhere and ALL curriculum fits into them in one way or another. There are an abundance of meaningful learning opportunities rooted in the local environment, whether built or natural. Keep an eye out for ways in which students can get involved and positively impact their communities in some way, big or small. You can use any local connection(s) you want, as long as they help give rise to relevant and authentic learning opportunities. Think global, act local!

Once more: we focus on *three major inputs* when using the C.A.R.E. method; these are:

1. Curriculum Outcomes (general or lean ones more than highly specific ones)

2. Global Competencies (the skills students need to thrive in the modern world)

3. Local Learning Opportunities (real-world opportunities and challenges rooted in the local community and environment)

As you read on, please continue to think about C.A.R.E. as a multi-content method which can handle even more inputs—we just start with these three for the purposes of learning together.

The method is quite adaptable. You will love it.

What Does C.A.R.E. Mean to the Classroom Teacher?

Using the C.A.R.E. method means you have a chance to focus on the authentic, relevant, and engaging learning of curriculum while students develop critical competencies through real-world learning experiences arising from your community.

What could be more authentic, relevant, and engaging than:

>> Making curriculum real

>> Proving students with opportunities to gain and practice critical competencies

>> Contributing to a vibrant local community and natural environment with which students feel a strong connection and have a desire to protect

And if this helps to get students motivated and engaged while decreasing behaviour problems, then all the more reason to get started!

Relevant Learning is Place-Based Learning

When we talk about learning that is authentic and meaningful, it makes sense for it to have a local component. After all, students are shaped by the culture, history and environment surrounding them in their community. There are always opportunities to make local connections and explore possible ways of making a difference on a local level.

> *"When they are anchored in both human and natural communities, people can experience a sense of contentment, meaning, and purpose"* —Gregory A. Smith

If given the chance to make personal connections with their community, students will be more likely to value and appreciate it, and want to make it a better place. They will take ownership and be more engaged in school projects with a positive impact on the place in which they live. In the long term, it will help ensure they become active, contributing citizens.

Assessment

When we describe the method, you will see assessment is critical to C.A.R.E. It is critical because it is central to the method. The guiding rubrics you will learn to create provide a central platform to use when you discuss progress with students, and they give students both formative and summative measures to achieve while developing the metacognitive learning (see Appendix B for a sample rubric).

There will be more on this in the explanation of the method. We just wanted you to know that assessment is central and extremely important.

Now we will move onto some background and tell you about the research that has gone into creating the C.A.R.E. method. If you are ready to get started and want to skip ahead to implementation (Chapter 8), go ahead. However, you may first want to know a little more about how all of this began and how the power in C.A.R.E. was discovered. It is up to you!

CHAPTER 6

Early practical experiences

STUART: I was fortunate to receive a full-year contract immediately after I finished my Bachelor of Education. Ironically, I was offered a position teaching grade 7 and 8 math at my former middle school. I came in with the highest hopes and ambitions of inspiring my students to live authentically, think expansively, and create bravely.

Within only a few weeks, I realized I was assigned an impossible task. I taught more than 120 students per day, five classes each with anywhere between 24 and 28 students. I saw each class for a total of 45 minutes per day before the bell rang and they were sent to their next subject. Within that short time frame, I was expected to teach students particular curriculum outcomes they had absolutely no input in. I felt so discouraged and overwhelmed trying to provide meaningful learning opportunities for each student.

The worst part of all, my students knew I didn't connect to what I was teaching them. They told me so. And they showed me through their behaviours. Most of them had deep respect for me and were not intentionally malicious, but they are kids and they *were* disengaged. There was no clearer sign that what I was teaching didn't resonate with them at all. Behaviour issues constantly distracted me from the lessons. The disengagement, of both the students and myself, led to serious burnout on my part and unfortunately my students suffered the impact. I was not at my best; I was just hanging on.

I knew I had so much more value to offer these students, but I felt trapped. I saw myself slowly becoming a cog in the system. I was perpetuating the very thing I entered education to change.

A SYSTEM IN CRISIS

Seasoned educators often tell me behaviour issues have notably worsened throughout their years in the profession. This problem affects the whole classroom and is detrimental to a school culture. Behaviour problems distract other students from learning and require teachers to spend precious instruction time on discipline and behaviour management. Most teachers I speak with say they wish they could spend fewer school day minutes on discipline. Moreover, they claim it is one of the hardest parts of their jobs. Heard and concurred, my fellow teachers!

To transcend the current teacher-student power dynamics, teachers must seek to understand what is happening in the minds of their students. Far too often, teachers perpetuate an oppressive pedagogy simply because they are following the dictates of their superiors and the rules of the system.

In this context, students become intellectually and emotionally disengaged from their teachers and the prescribed curriculum, which often manifests in behaviour issues—a student's means of communicating their needs are not being met. This is something I struggled with as students would often come to me voicing their frustration with our school's inconsistencies—on one hand we aim to promote individuality and sophisticated thinking, while on the other we expect students to conform to uncompromising school rules and complete coursework with no relevance to their daily lives.

My principal and I agreed addressing our school's overwhelming behaviour issues was a priority, so she established a new position, referred to as educational support teacher—behaviour (EST-B). The role was undefined, so I was able to use my creativity and autonomy to develop an alternative model.

BEHAVIOUR PROBLEM—NO PROBLEM

Through school-wide behaviour intervention tracking, we noticed a small percentage of students required most of the behaviour support (often in the form of harsh discipline). We eventually reached a point in our school where some of these students required crisis intervention support four or five times in a single day. Clearly these students were facing significant barriers to success and had self-destructive ways of expressing their unmet needs.

To address the needs of those high-frequency, high-need students, I designed an immersive ten-week pullout program. My intention with the program was to offer personalized education in an alternative learning environment. Along with increasing the choice and voice in what and how they learn, I wanted to offer these students an opportunity to become more compassionate and resilient global citizens.

Before commencing the program, I had each student complete a wellness survey to provide insight into their emotional and physical health. As a school we chose to focus on four of the statements from the survey, so I decided to do the same with these students. The four statements are:

1. There is an adult at the school that I feel safe to talk to if something is bothering me.
2. I have a choice in what I am learning.
3. I am interested in what I am learning.
4. I take time alone to think about what's important in life, such as who I am, and what I value.

The pullout program was designed to promote authentic and relevant learning opportunities with the hopes of sparking joy in the students by allowing them to explore topics that intrigued them. The inquiry-based projects tested the students' abilities to think critically and creatively and encouraged them to explore their passion in a way that would allow them to contribute to society in a meaningful way.

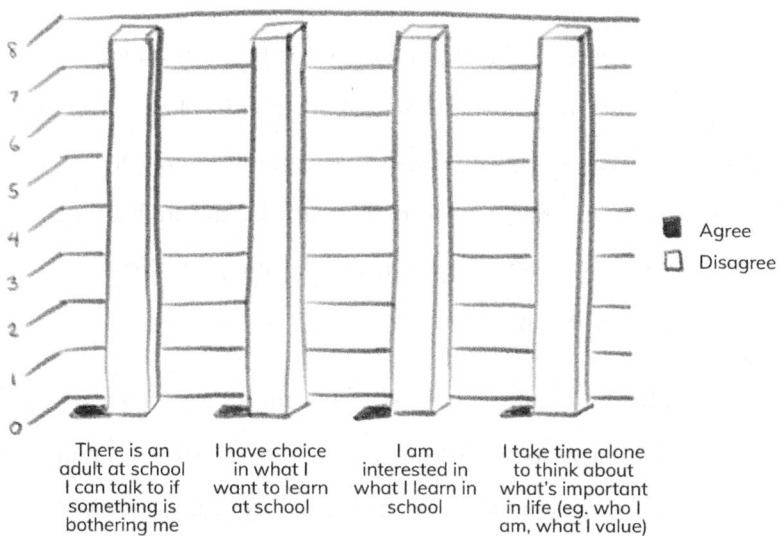

Figure 1: SLiC Students (Pre-Program)

Things moved very slowly at first, likely because students were not used to having such open-ended learning opportunities.

However, with guidance and encouragement, students came up with a variety of fascinating projects. Several students tended to a hydroponic garden where they learned how to grow and prepare food. One student established a school-wide recycling program. Another taught himself how to play guitar. One student taught himself how to code and created his own video games. Others chose to repair old bicycles with the intention of donating them to our local bike co-op.

These students continually amazed me in terms of what they can achieve when they are motivated about learning. Regardless of whether they are high achievers or struggle academically, I have seen students totally transform their attitude toward learning once they realize what they can achieve through authentic, relevant, and engaging projects.

The pullout program with the students only lasted for a ten-week period. Clearly much more time, effort and resources are required to ensure these students have the necessary values and skills to reach their potential. However, the difference in their behaviour and attitudes from start to finish was drastic. If nothing else, the wellness survey data demonstrates these students have a much better opportunity to learn and grow.

These students entered the pullout program with significant barriers to learning as is shown in the 'pre-program' survey answers noted in the graph above: not one of them had a strong relationship with an adult in the school; felt they had a choice in what they learned; were interesting or engaged in what they learned; nor reflected on who they are or what they value. These are essential conditions for a fruitful and inclusive learning environment. Yet, within ten weeks, all these students confirmed through their survey feedback that they finally had the basic conditions they required to engage in authentic, deep learning.

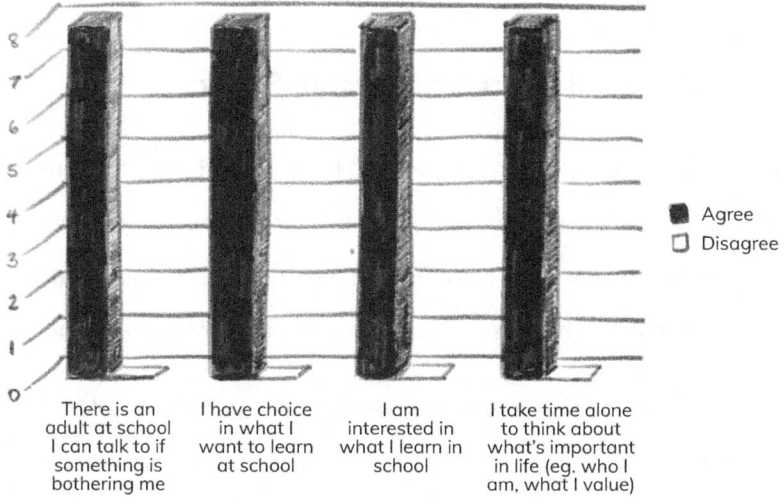

Figure 2: SLiC Students (Post-Program)

It is clear to me that students don't need to be filled with information to be successful; they need an opportunity to unleash their creativity with caring adults who encourage them to persist in the face of adversity.

Provincial Entrepreneurship Support

Following my time implementing the highly effective 'pullout program', I was fortunate to take on a provincial position supporting entrepreneurial learning throughout the province. In one year, I visited roughly 60 schools and worked with over 100 teachers.

I supported teachers in empowering their students to take ownership over their learning through action-oriented projects where they build their own independent business ventures and sell their products publicly.

Teachers mentored their students, helping them design businesses that address real-world challenges. It was amazing to see thought-provoking conversations spark curiosity, capture imaginations and inspire learners to flex their creative muscles. Students learned how to set goals, identify tools they will need and lay out a step-by-step action path to reach their targets. Essential competencies were developed through risk taking, experimentation, collaboration, and stretching their capacities as they implement their plans.

The entrepreneurial projects culminated in school-markets—dynamic events that gave them the chance to interact with customers and earn money. By donating a portion of their profits to charity, they also discovered the impact of giving. Throughout the process students reflected on their experience, celebrated accomplishments, and developed success strategies for school and other areas of life.

Everywhere I went, I witnessed inspired educators and engaged students. It never ceases to amaze me how these problem-based learning opportunities naturally create a flexible and inclusive learning environment which supports learners with a diverse range of competencies and learning styles.

Bringing It All Together

By the time I returned to the classroom I had a strong foundation in project-, problem-, and inquiry-based learning methods. I worked with an incredible group of grade 5/6 students and dedicated the entire year to projects and initiatives inspired by classroom discussions, student interest, and community issues. As I had expected from my experiences with these types of active learning methods in previous years, my students absolutely loved coming to class and made it well known. I even received emails from parents telling me how excited their child is about certain projects and initiatives and how grateful they were to see their child so engaged in their learning.

Throughout the year, my students launched projects such as three-stream waste separation for the entire school, community cleanup events, designing and building a food forest, designing and building their 'community of the future', and building their own bird house from raw lumber (yes, I taught them how to how to safely use carpentry tools).

I felt reassured in my approach because, using the C.A.R.E. method I could ensure my students were meeting curricular outcomes, developing their global competencies, and addressing real-world

challenges. Through the co-construction of competency-based rubrics (Appendix B), both the students and I were clear on the expectations for each project. I supported students in setting achievable goals, developing action plans, and monitoring their progress along the way.

The students were able to upload their work onto their digital portfolio whenever they felt inclined to share, which established an accessible means to share their progress with both myself and their parents. The conversations, self-assessment, and feedback were always meaningful and centred around the knowledge and competencies we outlined in the guiding rubric. My students understood feedback was only a 'snapshot' of their progress and was always subject to improve with their continued efforts. In the end, students created meaningful projects they presented to their peers, school staff, and community. Their sense of pride and accomplishment was priceless!

STUDENT FEEDBACK

As educators, we demonstrate our dedication to lifelong learning by attending professional workshops, taking masters level classes, and self-reflecting. However, we often forget to seek out suggestions from our target audience: students. There is no better way to meet the unique needs of students than by prompting them for feedback.

	Agree / Strongly Agree	Disagree / Strongly Disagree
I worry about the future of our planet	17	0
I want to do something about the problems of the world	17	0
I want to live in a healthy, happy, and sustainable community	17	0
I like my schoolwork when I can solve problems for my school and community	17	0

Table 1: Students' feedback using Likert scale

I was curious to hear students' thoughts on the work we had been doing in class and better understand their perspective. I asked them four questions on a five-point Likert scale, from 'Strongly Agree' to 'Strongly Disagree'. I also asked two open response questions:

1) What is education for?

2) Is it important we learn about our local environment and how we can help create a better world?

All students agreed, with the majority strongly agreeing, to each of the four questions above. Based on what I have observed in the classroom, their responses were not surprising. Though, it was interesting to see how many of them felt strongly about each of these questions. Every single one of my students worry about the future, want to live in a happy and healthy community, and want to do work that is relevant to their lives. I hypothesize the responses would be comparable with any student population surveyed.

I was quite inspired reading through the responses from the open-ended questions. When asked, "What is education for? What is the biggest purpose of education?"—14 out of 17 students

---

OPEN RESPONSE QUESTION 2
Is it important we learn about our natural environment and how we can help the world?

Highlight of Student Responses:
• "Yes! It's super important for people to learn about the local environment because it can help us make better choices and keep our world clean."

• "With recent problems I think we should teach the new generation how to fix things and even try to teach ourselves in the process. But to do that we need some form of helping hand and if we combine school and local environmental problems we can reach that goal faster."

• "If we don't take care of the world we won't be able to sustain ourselves. That's why we should take care of the planet."

• "We have done a lot of harm to this planet and we need to help it."

• "There is only one planet Earth. Let's take care of it."

mentioned education in a context of problem solving, self-improvement, or changing the world. These young people have now begun to see school as not only a place of learning, but a place of personal and societal transformation.

I also asked the question, "Is it important we learn about the local environment and how we can help create a more beautiful world?". All seventeen students offered an emphatic 'Yes!', with their responses revealing the need to make better choices and create a healthier future. They have all expressed concern, even anxiety, about their uncertain future. However, they are also hopeful because they are taking constructive action in their community—convinced they can make a difference.

We should take action so we can make the future better than the past and we can have a healthy life for every living creature.
— Grade 5 Student

INSIGHTS—UNPACKING MY EXPERIENCE

What have I learned? If we want to engage our students, we can start by listening to them.

That year, I was intentional about fully including students in the governance and decision-making processes in school, in the design of programs and learning opportunities, and in the civic life of their community. There were no behaviour issues (other than typical ten-year-old silliness), they continued their work at home without being asked, and they were self-organizing initiatives to make their school and community better.

There are few better ways to get students to deeper inquiry and connected learning than to have them engaged in real issues with deep meaning to them, their family, and their community.

Through C.A.R.E. I have found wonder in my students and have created the structures and conditions for their own authentic learning to occur. I guide, moderate, coach, and only teach traditionally for small parts of the content needed to further their learning. I simply show up each week and provide an opportunity for the young people I work with to cultivate and demonstrate their 21st century skills. Not information regurgitation, not standardized assessments, but a platform for them to exemplify their genuine leadership skills and deep learning.

Often, you will hear people talk about the need to prepare students for jobs that do not yet exist. I believe we are also training them to face problems not yet realized. If we want a future world where peace and prosperity become a lived reality, we must give the youngest of our societies the opportunity to become active global citizens, while granting them their right to be involved in the processes concerning them.

CHAPTER 7

How C.A.R.E. works

C.A.R.E. Components in Brief

The beauty of C.A.R.E. is that it consists of five simple steps you can easily integrate into any learning endeavour. C.A.R.E. will help take your teaching to new heights by organizing and refining practices you have likely been using to some extent already. Let's dive in!

STEP 1: Content Input: Clarify the desired learning outcomes by using multiple content foci.

Three fundamental pillars /inputs help narrow down the desired focus of learning:

» Global Competencies (GCs) → essential skills to be developed for success in the 21st century

» Specific Curriculum Outcomes [SCOs; or General Curriculum outcomes (GCOs), if applicable] → essential knowledge to be acquired

» Local Learning Opportunities (LLOs) → A 'lens' for learning that encourages students to think globally and act locally

** Note – Extra content (SCOs/community issues) will be added into focus organically through discussion, reflection, etc.

Cycle of Active Relevant Engagement
(C.A.R.E.)

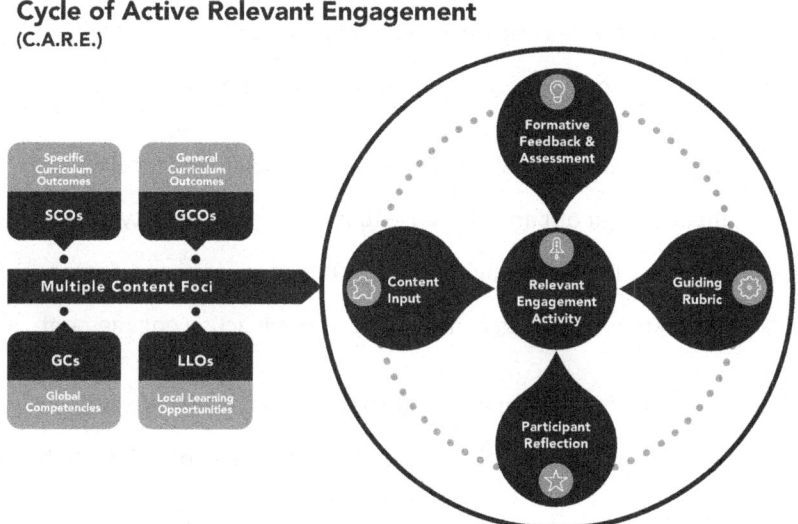

STEP 2: Guiding Rubric: Co-develop a clear, robust rubric defining key indicators and complexity levels required to demonstrate knowledge and competency of chosen content.

Governed by a rubric with GCs and SCOs as central, the student will demonstrate their knowledge and competency of each through self-reflection, formative feedback, and a culminating activity (presentation, product, outcome, etc.).

** Student / Teacher will be aware of the value to the local community of any activity undertaken.

STEP 3: Relevant Engagement Activity: Choose activities which will provide engaging experiences that integrate the chosen content through knowledge and skill attainment.

An opportunity, problem, or challenge based in the local community is sought out and gives rise to a meaningful activity relevant to the student and provides opportunities to learn and demonstrate knowledge and competency through active engagement.

The type of activity chosen may be inquiry-based, entrepreneurial, personalized, etc. It is imperative the activity be informed by and relate directly to the three C.A.R.E. pillars as outlined in the guiding rubric.

STEP 4: Participant Reflection: Engage and support students in reflecting on the rubric to guide their progress through all activities, along with their concurrent growth.

Through knowledge of the (i) GCs and SCOs important to this activity, and (ii) guiding rubric that governs demonstration of knowledge and competency, the student gains meta-cognitive leverage and becomes a self-directed learner.

STEP 5: Formative Feedback & Assessment: Provide continuous feedback to each student by using myriad strategies for the demonstration of acquired knowledge and skills related to the chosen content.

Through knowledge of the (i) GCs, SCOs and LLOs important to this activity, and (ii) guiding rubric that governs demonstration of knowledge and competency, the teacher, parents, community member (etc.) provides on-going feedback on progress and development as the student progresses through the activity.

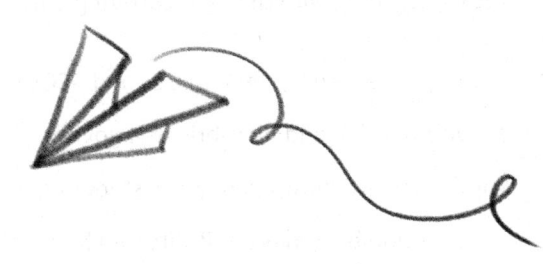

PRACTICAL APPLICATION

CHAPTER 8

Using C.A.R.E. step-by-step

C.A.R.E. Method Walkthrough #1

STUART: In this example, I will share how I supported a teacher in their first experience implementing the C.A.R.E. method.

The school is situated in a rural community with a food bank, but no grocery store. Many families rely on the food bank for sustenance. Over the summer, the teacher's school fund-raised enough money to install a massive 30 x 60 ft^2 geothermal greenhouse. This has been a huge project for the school as they hope to empower students with solving local food security issues.

With a general food security theme in mind, it was time to put C.A.R.E. in action! Here are the steps we followed.

1. Decide on content focus areas.

The first step was to decide on the multi-content areas we wanted to focus on. In New Brunswick, public education has focused largely on three main pillars: curricular outcomes, global competencies, and local issues. This may be different in your jurisdiction, but you can easily replace any of these foci with your respective area of interest.

Relevant and engaging experiential learning projects are cross-curricular by nature. When starting to consider learning outcomes to focus on, we could have easily filled a whole whiteboard with possible outcomes that could be met. For the sake of clarity and simplicity, we selected only a few areas of focus. This would allow students to concentrate on specific learning objectives and the teacher to keep things simple as they build their confidence with experiential learning.

Along with our 'food security' local issue, we selected two curricular outcomes that fit well with the content: science and social studies. We also selected two global competencies: sustainability and global citizenship, and communication. These multi-content foci provide more than enough opportunities to develop learning objectives for students.

Curricular Outcomes	Global Competencies	Local Issues
Science - Analyze and Explain	Sustainability and Global Citizenship	Address food insecurity in our community
Social Studies – Citizenship	Communication	

Table 2: Multi-content foci for learning

2. Co-develop a clear guiding rubric that defines key indicators and complexity levels required to demonstrate content.

Once we homed in on the specific foci, we were able to design a rubric (see pg. 82) that would provide key success indicators for students. While many school districts and departments still focus on frequency-based assessment (e.g.: how often a student does a student thing), we recommend complexity-based assessment, which emphasizes skill development.

We used our existing curriculum and global competency documents to design a development continuum. In the table on page 88, you will see the level of complexity increase from left to right.

We chose to leave the number grades off the rubric so students can focus on learning and receive authentic feedback without being caught up in getting a certain mark on their report card. (You are welcome to add grades to the rubric, if you prefer.)

Once the rubric was drafted, it was time to engage the students. We projected the rubric on the board and walked through each outcome with them. We facilitated a classroom discussion, asking the students to share their interpretation of each outcome. As the students put the outcomes in their own words, we typed the student-friendly terminology in the boxes.

3. Decide on activities that will provide opportunities to demonstrate content and complexity.

Once the outcomes and competencies were selected, the guiding rubric was designed and drafted into student-friendly language, it was time to decide on the activities students would do to demonstrate their knowledge and skills.

Using our 'Teacher Planning Guide' (Appendix C), I supported the teacher in developing specific milestones for the project, with the culminating piece being some form of product presented to the public. We decided the final product would be for students

Goals	Why	Circle where you think you are on the skill development continuum		
Research		Ask Open Questions (not yes / no answers)	Generates questions that lead to further exploration AND shows understanding of different purposes for questions.	Generates questions that lead to further exploration AND brainstorms solutions to problems
		Obtains info from reliable media (one source)	Obtains information from reliable media (at least 2 sources)	Obtains information from reliable media (at least 2 sources) AND locates main ideas in the sources
Share and Present (Language Arts)		Uses evidence to support an idea	Uses evidence to confirm or refute and idea	Uses evidence to confirm or refute an idea AND can make 'big picture' connections
		Shows understanding of project	Shows understand of project AND can make connections to bigger picture	Shows understanding of content AND can make connections to bigger picture AND can answer and elaborate on most/all questions asked
Citizenship (Social Studies)		Consider local perspectives on farming practices	Consider local perspectives on farming practices AND consults with local farmers	Consider local perspectives on farming practices AND consults with local farmers AND support a position
		Consider local perspectives on food security	Consider local perspectives on food security AND compare with Sackville (or other NB cities)	Consider local perspectives on food security AND compare with Sackville (or other NB cities) AND brainstorm solutions
Analyze and Explain (Science)		Uses evidence to support an idea (hypothesis)	Uses evidence to confirm or refute and idea	Uses evidence to confirm or refute an idea AND can make 'big picture' connections
		Gather data	Gather data using scientific methods (graphs, T charts, etc.)	Gather data using scientific methods AND determine what data is telling us

Table 3: Sample rubric used with grade 5 students

to grow their own plot of vegetables and share (using video, podcast, PowerPoint, etc.) their journey—what went well, what didn't, what they would change next time, and more.

Working backward from the final product, we were able to identify key milestones that would help guide students toward the end goal. When each of the key milestones were identified, we further broke each milestone down into days. We needed to know roughly how many days would be required for each step, what information or skills the students would require, and how we would like to gather formative assessment. This step essentially allowed us to build a calendar so we could know what would be coming up throughout the project and be prepared well ahead of time.

4. Engage and support participants in using reflection on the guiding rubric to guide their work.

AND

5. Provide continuous feedback as the participant develops their demonstration of content.

Steps 4 and 5 happen in conjunction and often simultaneously throughout the project. Once we re-created the rubric with the students (step 2), we now had common ground and student-friendly language that students could understand the project expectations and metrics for success.

Ultimately, we wanted to ensure we were able to develop a system where we could easily and effectively track the triangulation of data—observations, conversations, and products. All of this would be assessed and evaluated through the lens of the project guiding rubric.

NOTE: Digital or paper-based portfolios are an excellent option to help empower students in tracking their own learning journey.

We developed a 'Student Planning Guide' (Appendix D), which the students completed at the beginning of the project. This tool offered students a sense of direction and helped them take ownership of their learning journey. Additionally, we used a variety of exit slips, opinion reflections, goal setting and modification, and more to track student progress. This type of reflection not only put the student in charge of their learning and developed their meta-cognitive abilities, but also generated a tremendous amount of insight into how a student is progressing. We received constant feedback on which students require extra support and which ones could use a push to take their project to another level.

The culmination of the project ended with the students sharing their product with a public audience. For us, running this project during COVID-19, we had students create videos, podcasts, etc. showcasing their journey (failures, successes, learning lessons) and displaying them on the school's social media account.

NOTE: Students sharing their product publicly helps bring the project to life and encourages personal accountability in their work.

Once the project finished, we conferenced with each student. Prior to the conference, each student was asked to complete a self-evaluation of their ability to demonstrate content and complexity on the guiding rubric. The teacher did the same for each student. The two rubrics were compared, and this led to valuable and authentic conversations between the teacher and student. Once both parties agreed on the rubric evaluation, the student uploaded it to their digital portfolio and wrote one final reflection.

C.A.R.E. Method Walkthrough #2—A Simple and Adaptable System

STUART: As you will see in this second example, C.A.R.E. practitioners need not follow the method in a particular order. A more structured approach is recommended as you familiarize yourself with the C.A.R.E. method, but this example will highlight just how adaptable it really is. I have such deep trust in this method it frees me to be creative and free as a teacher. You will get there, too!

It began with a question to my students: "What are some of the biggest challenges faced by people in our community, country, and worldwide?". The response was delayed, but they looked deep in thought. This question sparked a two-and-a-half-hour discussion about a wide variety of challenges facing humans. Collectively, my students decided the most pressing issue is the environment. With the motto 'think globally, act locally' at the forefront of their brains, I asked them, "What can we do about it, here and now?"

After our investigation into the impacts of pollution on the planet, students were deeply concerned that none of our school waste was being composted or recycled—everything was buried in the landfill. This is the standard for public schools across the province. With more than 100,000 students enrolled in public education throughout New Brunswick, the tonnage of waste being unnecessarily buried is staggering.

Faced with an authentic and relevant problem, students were

hooked. The class decided to spearhead a waste management project, where they are converting the entire school to a 3-stream system (recyclables, compost, and waste). Students conducted a waste audit to get a sense of how much waste our school could divert from the landfill. They sorted the waste, weighed it, and calculated how much of it could have been recycled or composted. They were appalled to discover 70 percent of their daily waste could have avoided the landfill if they had a proper three-stream waste system in place.

They then consulted with experts in the field, including the Education Coordinator from ECO360, and researched about recycling, compost, and excessive waste. This made the 3-stream waste project a placeholder and provided direction for student projects. For example, they selected their own end-product to demonstrate their knowledge and competency, with the ultimate purpose of educating staff and students on proper 3-stream sorting. The projects varied from presentations and posters to puppet shows and a play.

Since my students were still relatively young and new to the problem-based learning approach, I scaffolded the learning experience by pre-designing a rubric for the students. At the beginning of the project, I shared the guiding rubric with students, and we went through together to make sense of it and put it in words they fully understood—everyone in the class was on the same page as to what skills and knowledge was expected to be demonstrated by the end of the project.

Throughout this active learning process, students were asked to self-reflect on their learning—showing where they were experiencing success, what they would like to improve, etc.—and my co-teacher and I conferenced with them on multiple occasions to provide constructive feedback. On a regular basis, often without being prompted, students were seen uploading their progress to digital portfolios and writing reflections about their waste management journey.

In their journal reflection on their waste management initiative, one student wrote, "The kids here really care about our future, and we are doing lots of work like cleaning up our community and starting a 3-stream waste program. We are trying our best and having lots of fun in the process!". Another student tells me their work is meaningful, they are trying their best, and they are having fun in the process. These are all fundamental components of a positive and constructive learning environment.

Now let's look at this same group of students and the start of their journey through the lens of the C.A.R.E. method, referring again to our trusty diagram:

Cycle of Active Relevant Engagement
(C.A.R.E.)

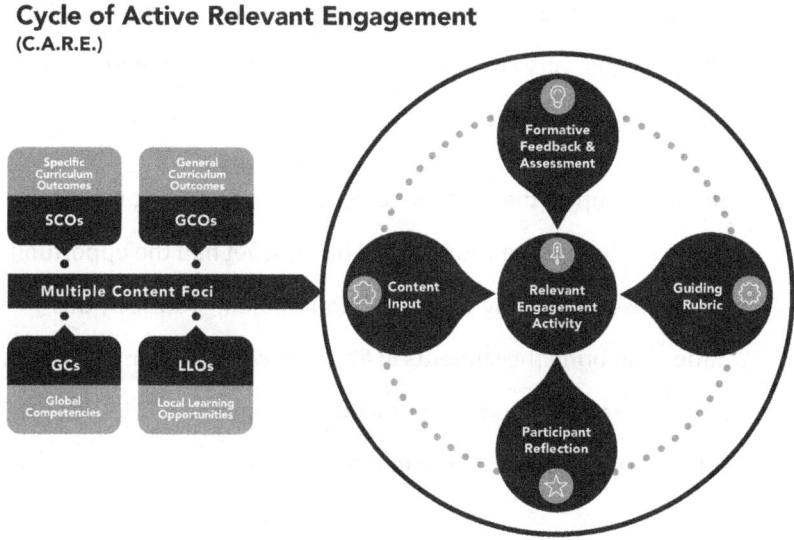

In the example above, because I had become so comfortable and adept with this method, I was looking for a starting point, something that would bring the students into a world of action and accomplishments, so I started with a question and a discussion. The discussion was rich and produced the results I wanted, but it is not necessary to start this way. I could have thought about a 3-Stream waste program as #3—a relevant engagement activity—and then built up the content input I wanted them to cover in terms of curriculum, global competencies, and a local issue. In this case, I did not go about the process in the normal way because I have become very comfortable with the model and have become very comfortable with students 'finding their own way' in my classroom.

In this example I then moved to developing the rubric myself, as these students were younger and had not yet had the opportunity to co-develop or individually develop a guiding rubric by this time. I did bring the students in #2—rubric-guided demonstration of competency—however, by talking through the rubric with the whole class and putting it into their language.

C.A.R.E. is so adaptable!

The beauty of walking through this method the way I did in this example, is I can prove to you that it works no matter where you start. And, more importantly, it provides opportunities for deep learning if you get all the parts of the method together in one project.

Let's continue to look at this example. You will note we used many opportunities to #4—Self-reflect—and as teachers we had many opportunities to provide #5—formative feedback and assessment—as we continued our journey.

The students did provide a group outcome of installing a 3-stream waste program at our school, and they did provide individual demonstrations of their learning throughout the project—i.e., plays, puppet shows, and power points etc.

The only thing left in this example is #1—Content input—and I should level with you as a reader. I am so confident with this model now that I knew I would cover the core curriculum and have students demonstrate some excellent global competencies while pursuing a relevant local issue. I built this step into the process of 'doing' so I could provide relevant content as students *asked* me to help them get the information they needed to develop the knowledge they wanted. This was a bit like the tail wagging the dog, and it worked!

CHAPTER 9

C.A.R.E. makes for deeper learning

AGNES: I had a wonderful opportunity to teach at a small independent learning centre offering homeschool enrichment programs. I co-developed a nature-based curriculum with interdisciplinary theme studies. Our year-long theme "shelter" lent itself to a wide variety of interesting topics and hands-on explorations.

We wanted students (7-13 year olds) to help decide the direction of our studies. We started the year off with a broad brainstorm of the concept of "shelter" in nature. Together, we honed in on the idea of habitats, what we knew about them, and the interconnections between animals and their local environment.

Through our brainstorming and subsequent discussions, everyone decided it would be interesting for each student to choose a local wild animal to research. They created a list of topics that ought to be included in their writing about their animal. This would be a long-term, in-depth exploration into their chosen animal, and would include using written resources; exploring the forests and fields surrounding our learning centre to gain insights into habitats and animal behaviour; having people that work directly with wildlife visit us to share information; learning skills like animal tracking, wild plant identification and primitive shelter building. The intent was to immerse ourselves in the shelter theme, learn about habitats in general, and our chosen animals in particular.

We educators wanted to be able to share students' findings with the broader community, and floated the idea of using puppet shows for this purpose. The students agreed creating a puppet show would be fun. In addition, it would be a means to share what students had researched in a meaningful, engaging way while weaving in interdisciplinary learning.

So, it was decided. Everyone would work toward the culminating goal of creating a puppet show (deciding later on how to divide into groups). Students got started on their research using the questions they had chosen to guide themselves.

Over the next few months, this broader animal research and puppet show end-goal was used to frame our explorations. Everyone had at least one animal they chose to study. They could decide whether to work on their own or in a group when using primary sources to gather information. They collaborated on writing short stories using story maps to prepare for script writing. Our art lessons explored themes related not just to elements and principles of art, but taught us to examine and create landscapes with a variety of materials and media—all in preparation for set design. The students sang and wrote songs and improv skits about animals and habitats. They built shelters using leaves, branches, snow and grasses—helping them understand how the local environment and the season shapes your home.

All in all, a great deal of engaging, fun and holistic learning happened throughout the year. And it was all taking us closer to the culminating end goal we had set out.

As an educator, it was fabulous to see the entire process unfold. The students were enjoying their learning and growing in many ways. Having nature as a second classroom all year long was not only important for helping students learn about their environment, but also to help them appreciate and connect to it.

The students' puppet shows were a huge success. They ended up splitting into two groups and creating characters based on the animals they had researched. Their sets were impressive and their props were fun. We videotaped the shows, since we wanted to be able to share them with families and the broader community. After many takes and some editing, the puppet shows were loaded online (the only time we used the internet the entire year), and everyone could pat themselves on the back for a job well done!

I will admit there a few hiccups along the way. Among them was that students were meant to use the puppet show to share their animal research. It was meant to be an opportunity to share information about each animal to help educate the public about local wildlife. This didn't really end up happening, as they had much more fun writing zany scripts wherein the animals had mad-capped adventures. Although the students gained immeasurable knowledge, skills and experiences from creating the puppet shows, the wider goal [of sharing what they learned with the wider community] was not met.

We somewhat remedied this by having each student write a brief summary of their research and share it through little one-on-one presentations. To decide what information was important to include, we looked to the original list of questions students had deemed useful to research. The resulting short presentations were video-taped and shared just with family.

In a roundabout way, we met our goal of learning about local wildlife through interdisciplinary discovery and then sharing knowledge through a culminating project. Thus, we considered the learning experience to be a success.

REFLECTING

Looking back now, with C.A.R.E. in-hand, I realise we fell short in one very important way: student reflection. Since we developed our own curriculum for our program, and since we were not doing formal evaluation—as one might expect in a more formal school setting—we didn't put much time into determining assessment tools. We accumulated a list of skills and competencies students gained through their explorations, and made observations we shared with parents. BUT, it's clear now looking back that students were not really included in the evaluation process. If only we had had a means to generate student input through asking for their reflections (in a documented way), I know we could have shaped the learning experience and outcome into something even more meaningful. The takeaways would also be a great help when planning future educational explorations.

As soon as I first saw the C.A.R.E. method, I knew it was an intuitive and valuable template to use for effective teaching. I think many educators use it already, to some extent, without having elucidated the steps involved. I typically teach outside the public-school system at small nature-based programs. I have no doubt that C.A.R.E. can take a curriculum—whether in the public system, private system, or homeschooling—and make it even more meaningful and interesting for students, and more effective and straightforward for teachers. Win-win!

If Only We Had C.A.R.E.

Hypothetically speaking, how would our months-long learning project be improved upon if I had had C.A.R.E. in-hand at the outset? Let's walk through the C.A.R.E. steps (keeping in mind we were an informal, part-time homeschool enrichment program with children aged 7-13).

1. Decide on content focus areas

Our curriculum this particular year was defined by the "Shelter" theme. It was imperative that any learning we did centred on local nature, wildlife and connecting children with the world around them.

Our student-centred approach of brainstorming to narrow down the content and topics fits well with the C.A.R.E. method. Students took the lead on narrowing down what they thought was worthwhile learning about without the broader theme. Our context was local and everyone chose an animal they were truly interested in researching.

2. Co-develop a clear guiding rubric that defines key indicators and complexity levels required to demonstrate content.

We did not develop a rubric to use over the course of our study, but I can see how helpful it would have been. We tasked students with developing the list of questions they wanted to answer through their research. They listed these in their notebooks and referred back to these throughout the research process.

Students were expected to work through the questions as one of the indicators of the progression of their learning. Once they had the information compiled, they worked in small groups and/or independently to bring their research to life through story-writing and art based upon their findings.

A C.A.R.E.-style guiding rubric would have helped ensure students knew not only the questions to answer, but the subsequent steps to follow throughout the course of their study. It would have guided them as they moved through the activities at their own pace. Definitely a missed opportunity.

3. Decide on activities that will provide opportunities to demonstrate content and complexity

I feel that our process, as it was, met the objectives of this step fairly well. Each activity we embarked upon—ranging from story mapping, to improv, to song-writing, to landscape painting and set design, to script writing—furthered learning and took us closer to our culminating end goal. Students had the opportunity to work on their own and collaborate with others throughout the process. Their knowledge of their animals, local wildlife habitats, landscapes and nature broadened greatly over the year. The activities were engaging, relevant and were centred in the local. Each student worked to their strengths, and grew in many ways. This was one aspect of our process that aligned well with C.A.R.E..

4. Engage and support participants in using reflection on the guiding rubric to guide their work

It was us educators who decided to go with the larger group project of the puppet show to present the culmination of their learning. This was certainly a fun idea, but in the future, I would want to have students co-construct the final project with us. This would make our learning better aligned with the C.A.R.E. methodology, and a more authentic, student-led experience. Maybe students could have brainstormed an even more interesting way to share their knowledge. It was a missed opportunity to not check in with them before deciding.

In addition, having outcomes and steps defined clearly in a guiding rubric for the final project would have also helped keep students on track. So, instead of puppet shows which were fun and silly, we could have had puppet shows that were fun, silly, and met our goal of informing the audience about each animal. We would have all benefited from being more organized from the outset!

Without a guiding rubric, our own reflections and those from the students were very informal and sporadic. Feedback was important, but was casually sought and not always productively integrated. On the other hand, using C.A.R.E. would have ensured reflections related to specific goals/steps, helping make learning more effective, meaningful and efficient.

5. Provide continuous feedback as the participant develops their demonstration of content

There was no shortage of feedback given by us to students as they progressed through their learning experiences. Given that our program was part-time and without expectations for formal assessment, we did not develop a complex set of outcomes upon which to base any assessment. However, their culminating project, as well as the products emerging from the other learning activities, were all indicators of learning, engagement and growth.

With C.A.R.E. guiding the process in the future, I would be sure to provide more regular feedback to students about their learning. I'd have more personalised conversations about what was working and what wasn't, and why. A rubric would help keep us focussed on what we were trying to achieve, but be flexible enough to jump on teachable moments that arose. We know students learned a lot during the year, but it would have been really great to actually have a better indicator of just how much growth occurred. Not just for ourselves, but to share with students and their parents.

To be fair, this was our first year of this learning program, so we were figuring out what worked as we went along. However, next time, with C.A.R.E. on-board, planning and delivery of our nature-based program will be even easier and more meaningful. We educators, as well as the students, will benefit from a more organized and well-thought-out learning experience that is fun, transformative and memorable!

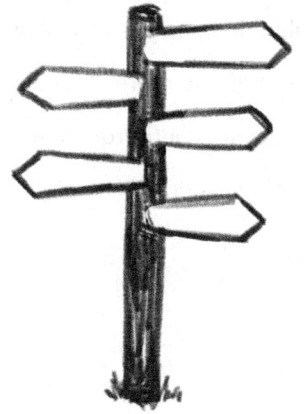

NEXT STEPS

CHAPTER 10

An invitation to get involved

Our reasons for writing this book are numerous. As educators ourselves, we are very excited about the C.A.R.E. method and all it has to offer. Not only will it make your teaching more effective and efficient, but it will help create learning experiences that are more meaningful and engaging for students. Making C.A.R.E. available to all teachers is important to us.

Education is constantly evolving. Over the years, there has been no shortage of new ideas and strategies teachers are encouraged to adopt. This can become confusing and overwhelming. It is difficult to know when to jump on board, or when to continue doing the "same old, same old". Nevertheless, the world around us is ever-changing and we can't assume that just because we've always done something one way, it's the best way to do it. We know many teachers would love to improve their practice, but are just unsure of the best way forward.

That is where C.A.R.E. comes in! As a proven, simple yet powerful method, C.A.R.E. can be the means to achieve the impact and authenticity your lessons may have been lacking.

C.A.R.E. makes it easy. Since you can start right where you are, with the same curriculum and desired outcomes you've already been using, C.A.R.E. helps you make the change today. We have no doubt that, once you start with this method, you will wonder why it hasn't been used in education all along. It's that intuitive!

We know C.A.R.E. has worked exceptionally well in myriad classrooms. Better yet, we are confident it will help take your own teaching practice to the next level.

So, where do you go from here?

Our aim is to provide as much guidance as we can to make implementing C.A.R.E. as straightforward as possible. The appendices that follow are a great starting point for using C.A.R.E.—there's no need to wait! We encourage you to get started right away and use this book as the stepping stone for integrating C.A.R.E. into every teaching adventure which lies ahead.

If you are interested in practical resources and support beyond this book, we are happy to let you know they can be found on our website (www.ihubcollective.com). We know the importance of being able to collaborate, communicate and problem-solve with other educators. You are invited to join our on-line community, where you can connect with others using this method in their own teaching.

We wish you much success and joy in your future teaching endeavours as you join the C.A.R.E. movement to take education to new heights!

C.A.R.E. diagram

The diagram on the following page provides a simplified over-view of the inputs and five steps in the C.A.R.E. method. Please see Chapter 7 for more detailed descriptions of each aspect of C.A.R.E.. Chapter 8 provides step-by-step walk-throughs to guide you through the process of integrating these five steps with useful examples.

Cycle of Active Relevant Engagement
(C.A.R.E.)

Guiding rubric

Use the sample table on the following page to help you design the guiding rubric for your next learning project. This particular example was used with grade 5 students. Modify the components as appropriate.

Goals	Why	Circle where you think you are on the skill development continuum		
Research		Ask Open Questions (not yes / no answers)	Generates questions that lead to further exploration AND shows understanding of different purposes for questions.	Generates questions that lead to further exploration AND brainstorms solutions to problems
		Obtains info from reliable media (one source)	Obtains information from reliable media (at least 2 sources)	Obtains information from reliable media (at least 2 sources) AND locates main ideas in the sources
		Uses evidence to support an idea	Uses evidence to confirm or refute and idea	Uses evidence to confirm or refute an idea AND can make 'big picture' connections
Share and Present (Language Arts)		Shows understanding of project	Shows understand of project AND can make connections to bigger picture	Shows understanding of content AND can make connections to bigger picture AND can answer and elaborate on most/all questions asked
Citizenship (Social Studies)		Consider local perspectives on farming practices	Consider local perspectives on farming practices AND consults with local farmers	Consider local perspectives on farming practices AND consults with local farmers AND support a position
		Consider local perspectives on food security	Consider local perspectives on food security AND compare with Sackville (or other NB cities)	Consider local perspectives on food security AND compare with Sackville (or other NB cities) AND brainstorm solutions
Analyze and Explain (Science)		Uses evidence to support an idea (hypothesis)	Uses evidence to confirm or refute and idea	Uses evidence to confirm or refute an idea AND can make 'big picture' connections
		Gather data	Gather data using scientific methods (graphs, T charts, etc.)	Gather data using scientific methods AND determine what data is telling us

Teacher planning guide

The project planning guide included here is an excellent starting point to help any teacher plan an upcoming learning project that integrates the C.A.R.E. method. Join our online community by visiting our website, www.ihubcollective.com, to access editable versions of this guide, along with other helpful resources for teachers. We're confident that these downloadable materials will help in the development of effective, engaging learning experiences in any classroom.

PROJECT PLANNER

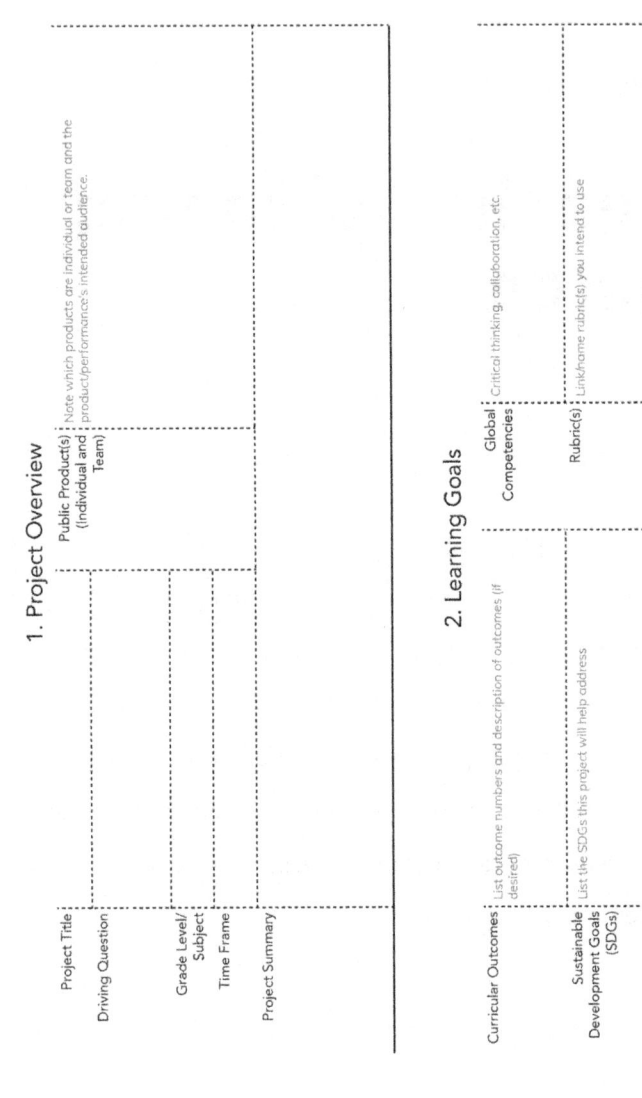

1. Project Overview

Project Title

Driving Question

Grade Level/ Subject

Time Frame

Project Summary

Public Product(s) (Individual and Team) — Note which products are individual or team and the product/performance's intended audience.

2. Learning Goals

Curricular Outcomes — List outcome numbers and description of outcomes (if desired)

Sustainable Development Goals (SDGs) — List the SDGs this project will help address

Global Competencies — Critical thinking, collaboration, etc.

Rubric(s) — Link/name rubric(s) you intend to use

3. Project Milestones

Directions: Use this section to create a high-level overview of the story of your project. Think of this as the broad outline of the story of your project, with the milestones representing the significant 'moments' or 'stages' within the story. As you develop these, consider how the inquiry process is unfolding and what learning will take place. The Project Calendar (Section 4) will allow you to build out the milestones in greater detail.

Milestone #1 Consider indicating if this is tied to team or individual learning/products	Milestone #2	Milestone #3	Milestone #4	Milestone #5	Milestone #6 Public Product
E.g. Entry Event	E.g. Student generated questions/research	E.g. Field observation and data collection	E.g. Feedback from an expert and revision	E.g. Finalization of product and preparation for presentations	E.g. Final presentation and reflection
Key Student Question	Key Student Question	Key Student Question	Key Student Question	Key Student Question	Key Student Question
This is the anticipated need to know question that guides the learning for the milestone.					
Formative Assessment(s)	Formative Assessment(s)	Formative Assessment(s)	Formative Assessment(s)	Formative Assessment(s)	Summative Assessment(s)
Identify how you will capture student learning to inform both teacher and student action in the project. These might be self, peer, or teacher assessments.					

4. Project Calendar

Driving Question:

Week: | Project Milestone: The calendar is organized by milestone so that you have flexibility when it comes to implementing. You may also structure by weeks if that feels more intuitive. A given milestone may take more or fewer than 5 days. Feel free to flex the form to meet your needs.

Key Student Question(s): This is the anticipated need to know question that guides the learning in each milestone.

Day 1:	Day 2:	Day 3:	Day 4:	Day 5:
See Section 5: Lesson Planner				

Notes: Include any notes that will help you with the implementation of this project milestone (e.g., resources, notes to self, etc.)

Driving Question:

Week: | Project Milestone: Duplicate tables for each milestone as needed.

Key Student Question(s):

Day 1:	Day 2:	Day 3:	Day 4:	Day 5:

Notes:

5. Lesson Planner (Supporting Resource)

How to use the document: This planner offers guidance on how you might plan your daily lessons in the project calendar. Pick and choose what feels necessary to achieve the learning outcome and advance product development for all students.

❖ FORMATIVE ASSESSMENT For each lesson, consider which assessment type best measures the learning outcome. For example, a quiz may be the best way to check for understanding of key terms while an annotated sketch might be best for determining student understanding of how the key terms fit together. In some cases, your assessment may be informal, such as an exit ticket, or more formal, as in a rough draft. Finally, when planning your formative assessment, diversify who is doing the assessment. Include self, peer, and teacher assessment opportunities, as appropriate for the age group. When possible, have external partners or end users provide feedback to improve or guide the work.

❖ MAJOR INSTRUCTIONAL ACTIVITIES This can include lessons, tasks, activities, or learning experiences. Choose the instructional method that will best help students achieve the learning outcome. For example, a direct instruction lesson may be appropriate for introducing the key players in World War II while an artifact inquiry activity during which students examine primary source documents would be better suited for them to understand the impact of those key players on the pivotal events during the war. This would also be the space to include teaching and learning related to classroom culture, student collaboration, and/or project management tools or skills, as appropriate for students or project milestone needs. Included links show examples of such activities.

❖ SCAFFOLDS Scaffolds are intended to be temporary supports that are removed when students no longer need them. These scaffolds can be used to support either content or the project process (e.g., need to know questions). Leverage "checking prior knowledge" to ensure you are offering the right scaffolds to the students who need them. Be sure to consider a wide range of needs, such as literacy skills, language acquisition levels, auditory/visual processing, building schema, learning style preferences, academic performance levels, etc.

❖ REFLECTION How will students reflect on their thinking, process, or learning?

❖ STUDENT NEED TO KNOW QUESTIONS ADDRESSED Which student questions will be answered, or are you aiming to answer, during this instructional activity?

❖ TOOLS/RESOURCES Student-facing tools, human resources such as experts or community members, teacher tools, equipment, etc.

Student planning guide

The student planning guide included here offers students structure and guidance as they tackle their projects and work toward becoming independent lifelong learners. Join our online community by visiting our website, www.ihubcollective.com, to access editable versions of this guide, along with other helpful resources for teachers. We're confident that these downloadable materials will help in the development of effective, engaging learning experiences in any classroom.

STUDENT PROJECT PLANNING

What is the GOAL of the project? *(eg. reduce waste going to landfill by introducing 3-stream sorting at our school)*	
What is MY PERSONAL PROJECT to help accomplish our goal? *(eg. presentation, drama, poster, etc.)*	
What kind of information do I need? Where/How will I find it? *(eg. website, ask parents, call local experts, etc.)*	
How will I capture my learning? *(eg. upload Planning Guide and regular check-ins on a digital portfolio)*	
What is my plan? **(Next steps... ex: start research for PowerPoint, plan the drama with classmates, design rough draft of posters/sorting guides)** **Make sure to include TWO check-ins with teacher**	**Step 1: Complete Project Planning Guide and check-in with (TEACHER NAME)** Step ____ : Step ____ : Step ____ : Step ____ :

About the authors

Dr. Leadbetter holds an interdisciplinary
PhD from the University of New
Brunswick in the study of high-performance teams and knowledge
conversion. He consults in organizational learning, the creation of
high-performance workplace culture,
and assists leaders as they learn to use the
C.A.R.E. method in classrooms, schools, districts, and corporate
settings.

Ross

Stu is a student of Life – always in search of eye-opening
first-hand education that only experience
can provide. He believes a more beautiful world—filled with abundance,
reverence, and possibility—is not
only possible, but is at our doorstep.
And quality education is critical for

Stuart

making this our lived reality. Stu is passionate about supporting fellow educators who share his vision in creating a new education system, where every child's innate curiosity, courage and capacity are nourished and strengthened.

A passion for environmental stewardship and finding beauty in the little things has led Agnes down a path of inspiring change. She has a Master of Environmental Studies with an interest in place-based nature education. Having co-founded two nature-based schools, Agnes knows the importance of tapping into every child's innate wisdom through joyful and empowering learning experiences. When not among the wildflowers, Agnes might be drawing or creating visual compositions for her graphic design company figdesign.ca.

Agnes

Made in the USA
Monee, IL
07 July 2026

56551425R00075